K is for Kindergarten

By Erin Dealey and Illustrated by Joseph Cowman

For amazing teachers everywhere and the kids they inspire, with special
thanks to Miss Zapp, Sarah Rockett, Mrs. Bedford, DW, and PRZ.
—Erin Dealey

For Mom and Dad, who taught me my ABCs.
—Joseph Cowman

Sleeping Bear Press™

2395 South Huron Parkway, Suite 200
Ann Arbor, MI 48104
www.sleepingbearpress.com

Printed and bound in the United States.

10 9 8 7 6 5 4 3

Library of Congress Cataloging-in-Publication Data

Names: Dealey, Erin, author. | Cowman, Joseph, illustrator.
Title: K is for kindergarten / written by Erin Dealey;
illustrated by Joseph Cowman.
Description: Ann Arbor, MI : Sleeping Bear Press, [2017]
Identifiers: LCCN 2017006067 | ISBN 9781585369959
Subjects: LCSH: Kindergarten—Juvenile literature.
Classification: LCC LB1169 .D43 2017 | DDC 372.21/8—dc23
LC record available at https://lccn.loc.gov/2017006067

Are you counting the days until kindergarten? Our **Kinder Countdown** activities will help you get ready! For kinders, teachers, and parents who want more, the **Kinder Challenge** activities are for you.

A

Kinder Countdown:

Are you ready? Have you circled your first day of kindergarten on the calendar?

Count how many days are left.

Make a paper chain, one loop for each day. Take a loop off each day as you count down.

Kinder Challenge:

Circle the 100th day of school on your calendar. Can you learn 100 words by then?

Make another paper chain by writing a new word on a new loop of paper every day. Soon you will have 100 words for the 100th Day!

A is for **At last**! It's happening.
Kindergarten's almost here!
You've been waiting for this moment.
Every day feels like a year!

B is for **bouncing balls** at recess.
Lots of balls to bounce and throw.
Bet you love to run and jump.
Kindergartners go, go, GO!

B

Kinder Countdown:

It's best to bounce or throw a ball outside! In kindergarten, you'll get to play outside at recess.

B is also for books. When an adult reads you a book, have them run a finger under each word as they read. You try it too! Words go from left to right and top to bottom.

Kinder Challenge:

Can you bounce a ball to music? One bounce for every beat!

With a partner, take turns bouncing the ball as you count. Start with one bounce, then have your partner bounce two times, then you bounce it three, and so on. See how far you can bounce and count!

C

Kinder Countdown:

What do you think your kindergarten classroom will look like? Have you visited a classroom before?

Draw a picture of yourself in your kindergarten classroom. What's the first thing you'd like to do when you get there?

Kinder Challenge:

Trace your hand on a piece of paper and color it. Around the fingers, draw pictures of your five favorite things about kindergarten so far!

C is for **crayons** and **coloring**.

How creative can you be?

Glitter, scissors, paste, and yarn—
make some art for all to see!

D is for following **directions.**

Can you follow these school rules?
1. Make good choices.
2. Use inside voices.
3. Do your best.
4. Respect is COOL!

Kinder Countdown:

Soon you'll be following directions in school. You can practice with a game called Hidden Treasure.

Have a friend or family member close their eyes as you hide a small object in the room. Then give them directions, step by step, to lead them to the treasure. Once they have found the treasure, it's their turn to hide it!

Kinder Challenge:

D is also for desk! Before Back-to-School Night, draw a map of your school. List the directions a parent or adult might follow to find your desk.

E

Kinder Countdown:

Everyone sing! Do you know the song, "Mary Had a Little Lamb"? Can you sing it?

Mary's lamb followed her to school one day. What pets and stuffies will you have to leave at home?

Kinder Challenge:

What would Mary say if she could share her lamb at circle time?

You might get a chance to share your favorite pet or stuffed animal with your class. When it's your turn, what will you share?

P.S. If your elephant is too big to sit on your desk, please leave him at home!

E is for **elephant**. Hold on there!
Elephants don't go to school.
Neither do our pets and stuffies.
Leave them home, please. That's the rule.

SCHOOL

F is for all the smiling **faces**
of the new kids that you meet.
Some may ride the bus to school.
Some might live right down the street.

F

Kinder Countdown:

Do you live close to your school or far away? How will you get there? By bus? By foot?

Make a chart of all the ways students might travel to your school.

Kinder Challenge:

Have you ever wondered how children around the world get to school? By ferry? Flying saucer? What types of transportation can you add to your chart?

G

Kinder Countdown:

Have you ever played school with your friends or family?

Dress up as the teacher. Imagine you're in class and your students have to raise their hand and wait to be called on before they can speak. (It's not always easy!)

H

Kinder Challenge:

Start a Wonder Wall. I is for what IF you could learn about anything that interests you? What do you wonder about? Write each wonder on a sticky note. Start with the words "I wonder..." Imagine the fun you'll have discovering the answers!

I

G is for **getting along** and **games**.
Kinders wait to take their turn.
H is **happy** sharing, raising **hands**.
I: **Imagine** what you'll learn!

J is for **jitters**. Are you nervous?

Just a little? That's okay.

Nerves won't last long. You'll make new friends!

K is for **kinder kids**-hurray!

J

Kinder Countdown:

Ask your family members if they remember when they went to kindergarten. What did they wear? How did they get to school? Were they nervous or excited?

Have them draw a picture of themselves in their kindergarten classroom—just like you did. How is it different from your drawing? How is it the same?

K

Kinder Challenge:

Shake, skip, jump! It's natural to feel some jitters before big events, especially when you want to do well. Shake your hands out or try to jump your jitters away. Skipping helps chase those jitters away, too.

L

Kinder Countdown:

Can you sing the ABC Song? It's a great way to learn your letters.

M

Kinder Challenge:

Make some music! Listen to a song like "Old MacDonald Had a Farm." Clap out the beat or use a drum. Can you hear when the pattern of the beats changes? The patterns you can hear in music are called rhythms.

KLMNOPQRSTUVWXYZ

L is for **listening** and **letters**.
A B C D E F G!
M is **music**. Let's sing together!
H I J K L M N O P!

N

Kinder Countdown:

Your teacher might give each student a number so you know how to line up when your class goes to the playground or library. Sometimes your teacher might ask the class to line up in alphabetical order, by first name.

What letter does your name start with? Where might you stand in the line? At the beginning? In the middle? Near the end?

N is for **numbers**. Kinders counting!

I bet you can count to ten.

O is for **outside**. P is for **playground**.
We love recess with our friends!

O

Kinder Challenge:
O is for opposites. Can you guess the opposite of each of these words?

day	laugh	go
hot	happy	bad
slow	tall	top

P

(Answers: night, cold, fast, cry, sad, short, stop, good, bottom.)

Q

Kinder Countdown:

The Quiet Game: Do you think you could play a board game or enjoy a stack of books without talking? Set a timer and try it for 5 minutes. How about 10 minutes? See if you can get through an entire game or stack of books. Each time you play this game, try to increase your quiet time.

P.S. Giggling is allowed!

Q is for **quiet** reading time
on the rug by the bookshelves.

R is **restroom**. Wash your hands, please.
Kinders go all by themselves!

Kinder Challenge:

All kinders should know how to use the restroom by themselves, and washing your hands is an important step. Saving water is important, too! Can you reduce your use? Next time, when you wash your hands, turn off the water and sing the Birthday Song while you soap up. Then quickly rinse and dry. It's a fun way to stay healthy—and save our Earth.

Make a poster to show other ways we can reduce our water use, and save the Earth.

S is **sleep**. All kinders need it
after long hours filled with fun.
Shhh. It's time for bedtime stories.
Stars are shining. Day is done.

Kinder Countdown:

Are you a night owl? If so, you may have a hard time staying awake at school.

Make a clock with a brad and construction paper for the hands.

Move the hands to the time you will need to leave for school. Have your family help you figure out what time you should go to bed on a school night, so that you don't miss out on kindergarten fun. Busy kinders have more energy after eight hours of sleep each night.

Kinder Challenge:

Who reads you bedtime stories? What if you are the reader tonight? It's fun to read to others.

T

Kinder Countdown:

What does the teacher have in the room? Can you find more...

T words: trucks, toys, tyrannosaurus rex?

U words: umbrella?

V words: vase of flowers?

W words: water bottle?

The alphabet is everywhere!

U

T is for **terrific teacher**.
U is **US**—her favorite class.
V is **very** busy—always!
W is **WOW**. The day goes fast!

V

Kinder Challenge:

Have you ever wondered what your terrific teacher was like in kindergarten? Ask yours to share a favorite kinder memory using all of the five senses: sight, sound, touch, smell, and taste.

Now you try it!

W

X

Kinder Countdown:

Make a time capsule to remember your first day of kindergarten. Reuse an empty plastic bottle or a paper towel tube. Put the drawings you made while reading this book inside.

You might want to add a list of the favorite things you did or friends you met on your first day.

Decorate the container and attach a note that includes the date to open the time capsule. (The date could be the last day of kindergarten, the last day of elementary school, or even high school graduation.) Store the time capsule in a safe place until it's time to open it.

Make a map so you can find it again. X marks the spot!

Xs and Os from all your family.
Y is **yippee**! Look at you!
Z is **zoom** with Kinder Power.

Every day brings something new!

Y

Kinder Challenge:

Make your own kindergarten alphabet. What words would you choose for each letter?

Z

Erin Dealey is a little sister who knows what it's like to count the days until school starts. She skipped half of kindergarten, so she loves to go back and visit. In sixth grade, she got to read to the kinders once a week. (Maybe that's why she became a teacher—and an author!) Her picture books include *Deck the Walls*, *Goldie Locks Has Chicken Pox*, and *Little Bo Peep Can't Get to Sleep*. You can find her at erindealey.com, as @ErinDealey on social media, or at school visits.

Joseph Cowman, although born in Westminster, Maryland, has spent most of his life among the mountains, lakes, and rivers of Idaho's Treasure Valley. He has illustrated numerous picture books, including *The Poo Poo Fairy*, *Noah Chases the Wind*, and *The Nutcracker's Night Before Christmas*. Joseph shares his Boise, Idaho, home with a school teacher (his wife), two daughters, a son, and a mischievous basset hound. When not illustrating, he can be found throwing a Frisbee®, slacklining, or skipping stones alongside the kids. You can find him online at josephcowman.com, as @Joseph_Cowman on Twitter, or as josephcowman on Instagram.